Cambridge English Readers

Level 3

Series editor: Philip Prowse

Just Good Friends

Penny Hancock

CAMBRIDGE
UNIVERSITY PRESS

PUBLISHED BY THE PRESS SYNDICATE OF THE UNIVERSITY OF CAMBRIDGE
The Pitt Building, Trumpington Street, Cambridge, United Kingdom

CAMBRIDGE UNIVERSITY PRESS
The Edinburgh Building, Cambridge CB2 2RU, UK
40 West 20th Street, New York, NY 10011-4211, USA
477 Williamstown Road, Port Melbourne, VIC 3207, Australia
Ruiz de Alarcón 13, 28014 Madrid, Spain
Dock House, The Waterfront, Cape Town 8001, South Africa

http://www.cambridge.org

Printed in India by Thomson Press

Illustrations by Mike Dodd

Typeset in 12/15pt Adobe Garamond [CE]

ISBN 0 521 77533 7

Contents

Characters

Stephany: a language teacher, lives in London.
Max: an architect, lives in London.
Carlo: a friend of Stephany's, lives in Genoa, Italy.
Ruth: Carlo's wife, lives in Genoa, Italy.
Luigi: a waiter.
Carlo's parents.

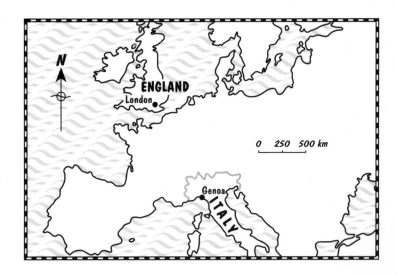

Chapter 1 *In Camden Town*

'I know where we can go on holiday!' said Stephany. She was lying on the sitting room floor of her London flat. There were newspapers and holiday magazines all over the floor.

All the hotels Stephany liked were too expensive. And she didn't want to spend her holiday in a cheap hotel with a lot of other English people.

Max came out of the kitchen with a plate of *sushi* and a bottle of cold Chardonnay wine. He knew this was the kind of food and drink Stephany enjoyed. Stephany looked up at the tall handsome man. His good looks made her heart jump.

The first time she saw Max, she thought he was a cold, unfriendly person. She could not believe that a person could be so good-looking *and* nice as well.

But now Stephany knew that Max was just shy, not unfriendly. He also thought about other people and tried to help them when it was possible. Stephany thought he was the perfect man.

He sat down beside Stephany and touched her black hair.

'Show me,' he said, nodding his head at the pictures of white beaches in the magazines.

'No,' said Stephany. 'This place isn't in the magazines. I don't know why I didn't think of it before!'

'Where is it? Tell me!' said Max. He was pouring the wine into two tall glasses.

'Carlo's flat!' said Stephany with a big smile. She took her wine and bit into the *sushi*.

'*Sushi*! My favourite! I love Japanese food,' she said. 'When did you get this?'

'I went into the supermarket on Camden Road on the way here,' said Max. 'I knew you would be pleased. Now tell me more. Who's Carlo, and where is his flat?'

'Carlo's a good friend. I taught him English five years ago when he was in London. He has a flat in a beautiful village on the Ligurian Sea in Italy, near Genoa. He said I can stay in it. I've been there a couple of times. It's perfect. You'll love it!'

'Slow down,' said Max. 'If it was five years ago, do you think he still wants you to stay in his flat?'

'Oh, yes, I'm sure. Carlo's a very kind person. He doesn't live in the flat now, it's empty most of the year. He only uses it for weekends sometimes.'

'Well . . .' Max didn't know much about Italians or Italian men. He didn't know if they really were good at being 'good friends' with women. It would be difficult for any man to be 'just friends' with Stephany – she was very pretty. He watched her now as she walked into the kitchen. She was just as pretty as when he first met her one night at the Jazz Café in Camden with some friends. They had been going out for two months now. Max had had a lot of girlfriends, but now he wanted to have a serious relationship.

It was easier said than done.

Some women were too interested in their jobs, other

women just wanted to have a good time. Some were too serious, others were not serious enough.

Stephany, however, seemed just right. She was intelligent and serious, and she liked her job. She was a language teacher and she worked hard. But she also liked to enjoy herself. She liked going to clubs and parties and doing sport. She did a lot of swimming and was very strong.

Max didn't really like sport. In fact he didn't like taking exercise. He was an architect and he enjoyed looking at buildings and paintings. But Max liked the fact that they were different and he liked her more because of it.

'I'm so pleased I thought of Carlo,' Stephany said, sitting down next to Max again. 'We'll have a great time. I love you, Max.'

It was the first time she had spoken so warmly. Although they had been going out for a couple of months now, she had never said she loved him before.

Max pulled her close to him.

'I love you too,' he said. They kissed.

Then Stephany began to describe the village where Carlo's flat was to Max.

'It's beside the sea. It's on Italy's north-west coast, near Genoa. The houses are built on the hills and are all different colours! And the country is beautiful – full of places where they grow fruit and vegetables. It's so pretty Max, and there are good restaurants with fresh fish, or you can get fresh pasta or pizza.'

'It's beginning to sound very nice,' said Max.

'We can walk, and swim, and water-ski . . .'

'Hey, slow down,' said Max. 'I can't water-ski.'

'Well, anyway, we can eat good food!'

Max put his arm round Stephany. He thought she was lovely when she was like this.

'OK, telephone Carlo,' he said, 'but not until later.' And he began to kiss her again.

Chapter 2 *In Genoa*

Some things never go away. You think they have gone. You continue with your life. You think, 'I'll never see that person again so there is no more need to worry'.

You have children. You go to work and come home. You shop for food and cook good meals for your family. You look after your husband well. You buy him trousers and shirts and ties. You make love with him whenever he wants it and say nothing when he doesn't. You don't agree sometimes, you think he might spend more time with the children. You know he works hard, and also know that the children can be hard work when he gets home. You put the children to bed yourself, although you have been working too. You are tired too, because you have also done the shopping and cooking . . .

This was what it was like for Ruth.

Ruth had met Carlo in Italy, when she was working in a restaurant. They had married, and she had left her own country and moved to live with him in Italy.

She had two children and they had lived in the flat in the village by the sea for a while. Then Ruth had wanted to move to a bigger house in the town.

The reason she wanted to move was to get away from Carlo's family. Carlo's mother and father lived in the flat next door and his uncle and aunt and cousins lived opposite. There was also a grandmother who lived above his parents. Everyone in the little village seemed to be part of Carlo's family!

Ruth couldn't get away from them. They seemed to watch her all the time. They told her how to cook, which fruit to buy, where to dry the washing . . . but she just wanted to be alone with Carlo and she began to hate Carlo's family. She had to get away.

Carlo finally agreed. He bought a house in Genoa because he loved Ruth so much, and he wanted her to be happy. They kept the flat by the sea for weekend visits and summer holidays.

One Friday evening the telephone rang. The children were in bed and Carlo was working late.

'*Pronto*,' Ruth answered, in the Italian way.

'Hello?'

'Hello.' At first, Ruth thought that one of her friends from England was ringing her. It didn't happen often. She felt surprised and happy.

'Hi . . . Ruth, it's Stephany.'

Stephany . . . ? Stephany . . . ? For a few seconds Ruth could not remember who Stephany was.

'Stephany!' said Ruth.

'Hi,' said Stephany. 'How are you?'

'We're fine,' said Ruth.

'How many children have you got now?' asked Stephany.

'Two. More than enough!'

'Yes. I think you're wonderful!'

'Wonderful? Why?' asked Ruth.

'Oh, bringing up children. It's hard work, I know, lots of my friends are doing it.'

'You haven't got any children yourself?' If Stephany had

children, Ruth would feel safer with her. She remembered the last time Stephany came to visit Carlo. It wasn't a happy time.

'Me? No, sorry! Not yet!' said Stephany.

There was a silence. Ruth didn't know what to say.

Finally, Stephany said, 'I actually wanted to know if the flat might be free in two weeks' time.'

'Oh no,' Ruth thought. What should she say? If she said it wasn't free, it would be a lie. If Carlo ever found out, he would be angry. She could say she needed to check with Carlo. But Ruth didn't want Stephany to think Carlo made all of the decisions. So she said, in a friendly and helpful voice, 'Why yes, I believe it is. Are you coming to Italy? Would you like to stay in the flat?'

'Well, yes, if that would be OK?' asked Stephany.

'Of course it would be OK,' said Ruth, although it wasn't true. 'It would be great. You know Carlo said you can stay in it whenever you want!'

So it was decided. Ruth put the phone down with a heavy heart – Stephany was back in their lives.

Chapter 3   *A good friend*

In London, Stephany put the phone down.

'Well, she seems to think it's OK,' she called out across the flat.

Max came out of the bathroom drying his black hair.

'Who's she?'

'Carlo's wife, Ruth.'

'Oh,' said Max. He was pleased to hear that Carlo was married.

'Great!' he said. He sat down on the sofa. 'I'll get the plane tickets.'

He held Stephany in his arms.

'I feel better for a shower. Now I can relax. It's been a long week.'

But Stephany couldn't relax. She stood up. Something about Ruth's voice had made her feel strange.

'I'm a little worried. I don't know Ruth very well. Maybe it's not a good time for them,' said Stephany.

'Oh, let's not worry now,' said Max. 'It's late and I'm tired. Let's go to bed.'

'OK,' said Stephany. But that night she didn't sleep very well. The next evening, while Max was cooking supper for Stephany in the kitchen, the telephone rang.

'Hello,' Stephany said.

'Hi, Stephany, it's Carlo.'

'Hello Carlo!' Max watched Stephany. She looked very happy.

'How lovely to hear your voice!' she said.

'Ruth says you want to stay in the flat,' said Carlo.

'Yes. If possible.'

'Of course you can! Are you coming alone?'

'No, I've met someone. He's called Max. He's very nice!' Stephany looked up at Max and smiled.

'Well then, we'll see you in a couple of weeks!'

'How are you, Carlo?' Stephany asked.

'So-so. Up and down. We worry about money, like everyone, and my wife is angry with me because I work too much. But if I don't work, we don't get any money!'

'Is Ruth working too?'

'Yes, she says she never stops working. She works in the day with the children and at night in a restaurant. But never mind. You come and have a holiday. It will be good to see you!'

'Yes, I hope we can all meet for dinner?'

'Sure. I'll see you then.'

'Bye, Carlo. And thanks!'

Stephany turned to Max.

'I knew it would be OK if I spoke to Carlo,' she said. 'He's a very good friend. He's really pleased that we are coming!'

'Shouldn't we offer to pay for the flat?' Max asked.

'No!' said Stephany. 'Carlo would be angry!'"

Chapter 4   *I don't trust Stephany*

'Who were you talking to?' asked Ruth, coming into the sitting room now the children were asleep at last.

'Stephany,' said Carlo.

'Why does Stephany want our flat for her holiday? Why can't she find her own hotel or something?' Ruth asked.

'You know I promised Stephany she could use the flat. It was before I knew you. I can't suddenly change my mind, just because we're married.'

'I just think giving someone my home is unnecessary.'

'But the flat *isn't* your home,' said Carlo. 'You didn't want to live in the flat, remember? You didn't like living in the village. You wanted a bigger house. This house is your home, not the flat. The flat is empty and it is much better if someone uses it.'

'You never asked me how I felt about it,' said Ruth. She knew she sounded a bit like a child, but she couldn't help it.

'I didn't know you when I made the promise,' Carlo said. 'I can't suddenly tell her she can't have it. If I make a promise, I like to keep it.'

Ruth knew this. It was one of the things she loved about Carlo. He was very honest, and if he said he would do something he always did it.

Ruth was always surprised that Carlo had married her.

She didn't think she was very pretty. Not like the Italian girls he knew, and she hated her red hair.

Carlo promised her he didn't like women just because they looked good and dressed nicely.

'One of the things I like about people from Britain,' he said, 'is they don't worry about fashion. Not like Italian women.'

Carlo loved everything to do with Britain: the sense of humour, the green fields, the people, even the food and the weather! The only reason he stayed in Italy was because he had a good job as a surveyor. But Stephany was from Britain and she looked good as well. Ruth felt jealous of her.

She didn't say anything more to Carlo about it. She went to bed. She heard Carlo go out. He had probably gone for a drink at the bar. Later on, towards midnight, she heard him come in again. The bedroom door opened. Carlo came in and sat on the bed next to her.

'Listen,' he said, taking Ruth's hand. 'You mustn't worry about Stephany. She's just a good friend. You are the only person I love.'

Ruth looked up. She was crying.

'And anyway, Stephany is coming with a new boyfriend!'

Ruth put her arms round Carlo. Perhaps things would be all right if Stephany had her own boyfriend now. She smiled at Carlo.

He was such a lovely man and she wanted to trust him. She did trust him. The trouble was, she just could not trust Stephany.

Chapter 5   *In a village by the sea*

Stephany and Max had ordered a taxi to take them across London and up the motorway to Stansted Airport.

'I love this building!' said Max. He was talking about the airport building. Stephany didn't say anything. It was something she didn't understand. To her, a building was a building.

However, she enjoyed being inside the airport with its shops that sold holiday things – everything from perfume to underwear and expensive clothes. She liked to watch the people too, lots of businesswomen on their way to Milan to fashion shows, and wealthy men on their way to expensive holiday places. She hoped that one day she would fly about the world earning lots of money.

Soon they were sitting on the plane. Stephany's stomach gave a jump as the plane took off, and she had her usual moment of feeling afraid as it rose into the sky. Soon, up above the clouds, she began to relax. The sun came into the plane. Max bought a bottle of champagne and they drank to 'our first holiday together'.

Then they were coming down, and the colours below them had changed from the grey and green of England to the gold and brown of Italy – the light was soft. Stephany had forgotten this about Italy. She came out of the airport feeling happy from the champagne, but also because she was back in her favourite country.

From Genoa they took a train down the coast. 'How do I ask for a sandwich?' asked Max. A man selling drinks had stopped beside them.

'Just ask for a *panino*!' said Stephany. She spoke good Italian and for some reason she thought it was strange that Max couldn't speak any!

They drank coffee and ate sandwiches as the train went in and out of tunnels and past views of beautiful houses, green trees and a bright blue sea.

'It's the next stop, I think,' said Stephany.

They picked up their bags and got ready to get off the train. A smell Stephany knew welcomed them as they climbed down from the train, a smell of the sea and of pizza.

They had to walk back a little way to reach the village itself. The colours that met them when they arrived were bright; pink and orange houses, red flowers and blue and green boats.

'Great!' Max shouted, and Stephany knew she had made the right choice for their holiday.

To get the key for the flat, they had to knock on Carlo's parents' door. The flat Max and Stephany were staying in was next door.

Carlo's mother, a small woman, stood looking at Stephany for a moment.

'Stephany,' she cried in Italian. 'You haven't changed at all. In fact, I think you are even more beautiful than you were before!' Stephany smiled and introduced Max.

The old woman was quiet as she looked at Max.

'Welcome,' she said after a minute, and then she disappeared into the flat and returned with a key.

'My husband has put a bottle of wine and some tomatoes and salad from his garden in the flat,' she said. 'Make yourselves at home.'

'Thank you so much *Signora*,' Stephany said.

'I hope you will eat dinner with us one evening,' the old woman continued.

'Oh *Signora*, that would be lovely,' said Stephany.

Max watched. He didn't understand what they were saying, but he thought Stephany was agreeing to eat with the old couple. He didn't like the idea very much. He wanted to have Stephany to himself this holiday.

Stephany continued to talk to Carlo's mother as if she were the most important person in the world to her.

'Has Carlo been here lately?' asked Stephany.

'He was here at the weekend and told me you were coming,' said the *Signora*. 'He asked Ruth to prepare the flat for you.'

'And how is Ruth?' asked Stephany quietly.

'So-so,' she said. It was clear from her face that she did not have much time for her daughter-in-law. 'She is always busy. I never see my grandchildren any more.'

'Oh dear,' said Stephany. 'I'm sure they love seeing you.'

The old woman smiled at Stephany.

Stephany then thanked the *Signora*, and led Max to the door of their flat.

'She likes you,' Max said, giving Stephany a kiss. 'I expect she hoped Carlo would marry you, instead of Ruth.'

'Don't be silly, Max,' said Stephany. 'She likes me because I was Carlo's teacher. Look, this is our bedroom.'

'It looks very nice,' said Max. 'Who did all this work?

Look, they have even put flowers on the table.'

'It was Ruth,' said Stephany.

'She's very kind,' said Max. 'She doesn't know us. And we are staying in her flat for nothing.'

'Carlo's flat,' Stephany said quickly.

'Yes, but as they're married, it's her flat as well. It's very kind of both of them, I'm sure we should offer to pay for it.'

'I wouldn't worry about that,' said Stephany. 'As I said, Carlo and I have always had this agreement.'

Max felt a little uncomfortable about being given a beautiful holiday flat for nothing. Stephany opened the windows and they looked out at a view across roofs to the Mediterranean.

'Wonderful!' said Max.

'And we have a balcony,' said Stephany, opening the doors onto a little balcony, where she shut her eyes and took a deep breath of sea air.

'Oh, the smells here are so good!' Stephany said. 'I already feel better. Let's unpack and go and get an ice cream from the *Gelateria*, and see if anyone's swimming down on the beach.'

'Good idea,' said Max, looking at Stephany in the Italian light. She looked beautiful and he thought that he really was in love this time.

Chapter 6 *The two couples meet*

The next day, Stephany and Max ate breakfast in the bar. It was only a short walk from their flat. They ate cakes and drank coffee. Then they went to swim at the beach at the bottom of the village.

'This certainly is an ideal place for our holiday,' said Max.

'I told you!' said Stephany.

'And if we had paid for a place like this it would have cost a lot of money,' Max said. But Stephany was changing into her bikini and didn't answer.

'Let's swim!' she called to Max. Before he knew it, she had run into the water and was swimming out to sea.

The blue water was clear and deep. However, Max chose to swim close to the beach. He didn't feel safe in deep water he didn't know.

Some local boys were diving off the rocks. They looked very healthy, as if they spent every day sitting in the sun, diving and swimming. Max thought of his white English skin and felt shy.

Stephany swam like a fish. Before long, she too had climbed the high rocks.

'Come up here!' she called down to Max. Max looked up at her. She had a lovely healthy body.

'I'll just stay here,' he called up. He thought he heard one of the boys laugh.

He watched as Stephany dived smoothly into the water. She swam up to him and took his hand.

'You're frightened to dive!' she laughed. 'Come on, I want to see you dive.'

'No,' said Max. 'I'm hungry. Let's go and get some lunch. I noticed one of those bars did large plates of pasta!'

'That's the *trattoria* – the restaurant,' said Stephany. 'Yes, that's a good idea. I'm really hungry after all this swimming!'

Soon they were dressed and sitting in the *trattoria*. People were ordering big meals, even though it was only one o'clock.

'People eat a lot at lunchtime here!' Max said.

'We've forgotten how to eat well in England,' said Stephany. 'Italians love their food. Just think, at home we would just be eating a sandwich!'

'But here, it's *spaghetti alle vongole*, and wine, and steak,' said Max, smiling. 'This is a great place,' he continued. 'Sun, clean sea, good restaurants. You were very clever to think of it. I'm looking forward to meeting Carlo and Ruth so I can thank them properly.'

But Max was also a little worried that Carlo might look like one of the boys on the beach, a handsome Italian with brown skin and strong muscles!

They returned to the flat much later, after their big lunch and a good coffee. There was a message from Carlo's mother, saying Carlo had telephoned. He wanted all of them to go out for a pizza together.

'He'll come to your flat at seven o'clock,' the old woman told Stephany.

'Hmm,' said Max, coming up behind Stephany and putting his arms round her. 'It'll be good to meet your Italian friends at last.'

'Yes,' said Stephany. But her face, which he saw in the mirror, looked worried.

'What's the matter?' Max asked. 'Aren't you looking forward to seeing them?'

'Of course I am,' said Stephany. 'At least, I'm looking forward to seeing Carlo. He's like my brother, but I'm not so sure about Ruth. I don't know her very well.'

'Are you frightened of her?' asked Max.

'Frightened? No!' said Stephany quickly. 'I just don't know her, that's all. And you know women with children can be very boring.'

'Boring?' Max said, surprised. 'Surely, some are boring, and some aren't, just like people without children?'

But Stephany pushed away from his arms and went into the bathroom to have a shower.

'I need to start getting ready if we are eating with them tonight,' she said from the bathroom. And the door shut.

Max went out onto the balcony and sat on a chair. He felt the warm sun on his face, and heard the soft sounds of the village around him. He closed his eyes.

He was woken from a deep sleep by the sound of someone knocking on the door of the flat. He looked up, wondering where Stephany was. He couldn't see her, so he went and opened the door.

A medium height, well-dressed Italian man with a friendly face and glasses stood at the door. He wore a clean white shirt and trousers, and had a pullover around his shoulders. With him was a small, red-haired woman with a white face and a baby in her arms. Holding onto her legs was a small child.

'*Ciao!*' said the man. 'I'm Carlo. This is my wife Ruth, and you must be Max.'

Max smiled and shook Carlo's hand.

'Well,' thought Max, 'I don't have to worry that Carlo is better-looking than me. I think I'm more handsome than he is!'

Carlo looked nice, but he was nothing like the boys on the beach. He looked like a simple family man. He probably ate too much pasta and didn't exercise much!

As the family came into the flat, the bathroom door opened and Stephany came out, looking more attractive than Max had ever seen her. She wore a short black dress which made her look very slim and high black shoes. Her skin was brown from their morning in the sea and sun and her hair shone like glass. And with the make-up she had put on her face she looked beautiful. Max watched her as she walked across the room and took Carlo's hand, kissing him on each cheek. Max wondered how Ruth felt.

Just then, the baby in Ruth's arms began to cry. She went to the bedroom to feed it.

'Shall we go to the bar?' said Stephany, looking from one man to the other, enjoying the fact they were both looking at her.

'Wait a minute,' said Max. 'Ruth is feeding the baby, remember?'

'Oh, she can find us there later,' said Stephany. 'She could be a long time feeding.'

'Why don't we have a drink here while we wait?' said Max.

He didn't know much about having children, but he thought it must be hard to be left out of things just because you had a baby.

'OK,' Carlo said. 'I hope you like it here. While you are in my flat it is your home.'

'Yes,' said Max. 'It's very kind of you. Thank you very much.'

Carlo looked at Stephany as he said, 'I always said Stephany can stay in my flat whenever she likes. And, of course, since you are her friend, you are also welcome.'

Stephany smiled at Carlo.

Soon after, Ruth came out of the bedroom. She looked white and tired next to Stephany, and there were lines on her clothes, a cotton skirt and a yellow T-shirt, from sitting on the bed.

'Would you like a drink?' Max asked her, and she smiled.

'Come on,' said Carlo. 'Let's go! We can have a drink in the bar.' And he led them all to the door.

Chapter 7   *A difficult dinner*

'Could you please watch Thomas?' Ruth asked Carlo as they sat down at a table in a bar. The little boy had run off and was throwing salt on the ground.

'Relax,' Carlo said to Ruth. Max could see that Ruth was getting angry. She got up with the baby in her arms and went and took the small boy's hand and pulled him back to their table.

'He needs someone to watch him,' she said, looking angrily at Carlo.

But Carlo was talking to Stephany. Max watched Carlo and Stephany. They were laughing together happily. Stephany turned to Max.

'Last time I was here Carlo taught me to water-ski!' she said. Her eyes were happy. Max began to feel a tiny bit angry. Stephany knew he couldn't water-ski. Was she trying to make him jealous? Or perhaps she was trying to make Ruth jealous. She seemed to be doing a good job.

'Carlo!' Ruth was shouting at him. The little boy had run out of the door of the restaurant and down the street.

Carlo said, 'You know my mother offered to take care of him.'

'I want Thomas to eat with us,' said Ruth.

'Relax and let him play, then,' Carlo said.

Just then the baby started crying.

Ruth got up.

'I think I'll go home if you don't mind,' she said. 'I can't look after Thomas and the baby in a restaurant without any help.' Her face was red.

She looked as if she was about to cry.

No-one moved as she got up, holding the baby in one arm, the small boy's hand in the other.

Max began to feel very angry. Why didn't Carlo help Ruth?

He was also angry with Stephany. She should understand how Ruth felt.

'Don't go,' Max said to Ruth. 'I'll take Thomas for a walk until his food arrives. We'll go and see the boats, shall we Thomas?' The little boy looked at him for a few seconds then held out his hand.

'Thank you, Max,' said Ruth. She smiled at Max. She had relaxed.

'You have your drink,' Max said, 'and I'll be back in a minute.' He walked down the narrow street with the little boy's small hand in his. They got to the beach where some people were putting a boat into the water.

The little boy stood and watched. Though he must have seen all this hundreds of times before, he seemed very interested.

'Do you like boats?' Max asked. He didn't really know what to say to children.

'*Sì*,' Thomas replied. Then he said something else in Italian.

How wonderful, Max thought, that a young child can understand English but reply in Italian. And I can't understand a word he says. Apart from '*sì*'.

The little boy said something in Italian again.

Max smiled at him. The little boy looked at Max, trying to understand why he didn't reply to him. Then he smiled. It seemed he understood suddenly that Max only spoke English.

'Let's see the fish,' he said in English, and Max, smiling, said, 'Yes, let's . . .'

They walked beside the water. Some men in a small fishing boat were taking some fish off the boat. The fish were silver in the evening light and a small crowd stood round the boat.

Max and Thomas were enjoying themselves so much they almost forgot the time. They went back to the restaurant. Max felt pleased that the little boy had trusted him. He hoped Stephany had seen what he did. If he couldn't water-ski, at least he could show her what a good father he would be!

'He's a sweet kid,' Max said to Carlo.

'When he's not being bad,' Carlo said and gave the boy a kiss. Max sat down. The baby was asleep. Ruth was drinking some beer. Things were going to be all right after all. They talked about everyday, ordinary things.

'What do you do Max?' asked Carlo.

'I'm an architect,' said Max.

'That's interesting, I work with quite a few architects,' Carlo said. 'I'm a surveyor.'

Stephany tried to talk to Ruth, but Ruth didn't say much to Stephany.

Thomas was playing a game with Luigi the waiter. The waiter was making paper hats and putting them on Thomas's head. Luigi was laughing. He seemed to enjoy playing with children.

'It must be hard work with two children,' Stephany said.

'It is,' said Ruth. 'In some ways I find it harder living here in Italy.'

'But the Italians love children,' said Stephany. 'I mean, look, the waiter is very kind to Thomas. In England, people don't like seeing children in restaurants.'

She didn't add that she understood why.

'I know, they're wonderful with him,' said Ruth. 'But if your own family isn't here, it's hard. There are not so many places for mothers and children to meet each other.'

'You've got Carlo's family,' said Stephany. 'They're lovely people. I love his mother. We get on very well.'

'Hmm,' said Ruth. 'It's a bit different living here.'

'I'd love to live here!' said Stephany. 'It's so beautiful with the sea and the sun and the lovely people. You're very lucky!'

Ruth looked at her. 'She has no idea what it's really like,' she thought. 'How can she call me lucky, when she has a good job, a handsome boyfriend, and she's free? And she is so good-looking. Carlo was probably in love with her. Perhaps he still is!'

But she said none of this.

'I've an idea,' Carlo said suddenly. Luigi the waiter was picking up their plates as they were getting up to leave.

'We could all go to the festival tomorrow night up in the mountains. It's a special day in a village. There'll be a party with food and wine and dancing. It'll be fun! Won't it Ruth? We went last year and had a very good time.'

'Yes,' said Ruth.

'Oh, it sounds great, doesn't it?' Stephany said to Max.

29

But Max was silent. He didn't know if he was going to spend any evenings of this holiday alone with Stephany.

Chapter 8   *A long way from the truth*

Max woke in the night feeling sick. In the morning he felt so sick he couldn't get out of bed.

'Wouldn't you feel better if you got up and came for a swim?' Stephany asked. She felt a little angry that Max was sick. It was so English to be sick in a foreign country.

'No, I wouldn't,' said Max, who just wanted to sleep.

'Well, I'm going to have breakfast in the bar, then I may go and swim,' said Stephany.

'You're not a very good nurse,' Max said, weakly.

'That's because I'm not a nurse,' said Stephany. This was not what she had come on holiday for. She wanted to have some fun. But on this holiday she had only discovered Max's weaknesses: he couldn't speak any Italian, he couldn't water-ski or dive or do any of the things the local Italian men enjoyed doing. Now he was sick, and she had to spend the day alone.

She left Max in the dark room and went along to the bar. The waiter brought her a cappuccino.

'Aren't you Carlo's friend?' the waiter asked, giving her the coffee. Stephany looked at him. She remembered him from last night. Then she thought she had met him the last time she had been here.

'Yes, I am,' she said. 'Sorry, but I don't remember your name.'

'I'm Luigi,' said the waiter. 'Carlo's one of my oldest

friends. We all went out together one night, about two years ago. Remember?'

Stephany felt her face go red. That night two years ago! She remembered clearly, but she didn't think anyone else would.

'Carlo liked you very much,' said Luigi. 'We thought he would leave his wife and marry you!'

Stephany looked at Luigi. She didn't know if he was being friendly or not. What did he know? And what did he really think?

'And his mother liked you too,' he said.

He smiled, and put his hand into his pocket to find change for the money she had given him for the coffee.

'And now you've got a free holiday flat. People pay a lot of money to stay here for just one week,' he said.

What was he saying? Stephany felt herself go hot. Was he saying she had made love with Carlo so that he would let her stay in the flat for nothing? It wasn't true.

She had just had a very short affair with Carlo last time she was here. He had already offered her the use of his flat a long time before they ever had that little affair.

She had hoped no-one knew and that it would be forgotten by everyone except Carlo. Discovering that Luigi knew made her feel very uncomfortable. She left the bar and walked along the beach, deep in thought.

She found a quiet place and went and sat in the sun. After a while she dived into the water and swam. But she couldn't relax. She felt bad because some of the things that Luigi had said were half true. She thought about the things that had happened two years ago.

She remembered seeing how happy Carlo and Ruth were

32

together, and feeling afraid that she was going to lose Carlo as a friend. Surely, she had thought, she was more interesting to him than Ruth. Although she had never found Carlo attractive before, she suddenly wanted him now he was married.

She remembered how she had gone out one evening with some of Carlo's friends, including Luigi. They had gone to a beach called Bianca Beach. Ruth had stayed at home.

She remembered how they had dived off the rocks and swam in the night water. She remembered the moment she and Carlo had found themselves alone, or so they thought. She remembered how they had kissed, with the dark water around them.

Afterwards, Carlo had said they must never let it happen again, because he loved Ruth. He would always be Stephany's friend, he said, but he didn't want to lose Ruth.

'We'll continue as if nothing happened,' said Carlo. And Stephany, pleased that he found her attractive, agreed.

It's simple, she had told herself. But that was a long way from the truth.

Chapter 9   *On Bianca Beach*

Max was still ill that evening. When Carlo came to take them to the festival Ruth wasn't with him.

'Thomas isn't feeling well either,' he told Stephany, 'so Ruth said she would stay and look after him.'

'So, it's just you and me,' said Stephany.

'Perhaps we'd better forget it,' said Carlo.

Stephany had been looking forward to this evening. With Max ill, she had had a boring day on her own. The things Luigi the waiter had said to her had made her think. This would be a good opportunity to talk to Carlo alone, although she wasn't sure how she was going to begin to talk about the subject.

It would be difficult to say, 'Luigi thinks I made love with you so I could have your flat, but it's not true.' She wasn't sure what she was going to say.

'Come on,' she said. 'Why don't we go? Just you and me? I need to get out. Max has been ill all day.'

Carlo looked at her. He found her very attractive, but he wished he didn't. He worried about being alone with her. His mother always said he should have married Stephany, not Ruth.

But Stephany had never been interested in him until that time two years ago. And by then he was married to Ruth and he loved Ruth a lot. He and Stephany had been friends until that time two years ago, so they could be friends again now.

'Well . . . yes, we could go,' said Carlo. He wasn't too sure.

'Good,' said Stephany.

Max was still asleep when they left.

They drove up a road through the mountains. There were trees on either side and when they came to corners, they could see views of the deep blue sea far below.

'I was thinking,' said Stephany, 'Instead of the festival, could we go to that lovely beach?'

'Which one?' Carlo asked.

'The one with the white sand and the pine trees. I think it's called Bianca Beach. It's where we went last time I was here.'

Carlo didn't answer immediately. He was remembering. They drove in silence for a few minutes before he looked at her.

'OK,' he said.

'Are you all right?' Stephany asked him. 'You're very quiet.'

'I was just thinking how things change,' he said. 'Now I'm a married man with children, I don't often find myself alone with a woman.'

'I'm not going to bite you!' laughed Stephany. But somewhere deep inside him, Carlo felt that was exactly what she was going to do. Soon they arrived at the beach she had talked about. Carlo stopped the car and got out. He came round and opened her door for her. She got out too. With the waves, the white sand, and the wind in the trees the beach looked beautiful.

'Stephany,' he said, 'that night two years ago was a mistake, you know.' Stephany looked at him. So he had been thinking about it too, she thought.

'I know,' she said.

'We can still be friends, can't we?' she said.

'I'm not sure,' Carlo said. 'The trouble is, Ruth doesn't feel very happy about you using the flat.'

Stephany looked at Carlo. She realised how much he loved Ruth, but she couldn't help feeling a bit jealous. Surely she was more attractive to him than Ruth?

'But you feel happy about it, don't you?' she asked, softly. 'Until you married Ruth, you wanted me to come here often.'

'Things are different now . . .' he said, then was silent. It was impossible to tell Stephany she couldn't come any more. It would be wrong of him. He hated breaking promises.

Stephany put her hand up to Carlo's cheek and touched it. Before he knew it, she was touching his neck. Against his wishes, he was finding himself attracted to Stephany again. This had been such a hard time for him, with Ruth tired all the time with the children. Suddenly, finding himself alone with Stephany like this, he couldn't stop himself.

Stephany felt Carlo moving as she touched him. She thought of Max, sick in bed, and Ruth, at home with two children. She thought of Luigi in the bar. But suddenly none of this seemed to matter. She was kissing Carlo wildly, and they pulled off each other's clothes. They fell onto the sand, which was still warm from the sun, and lay together as the moon came up.

As they drove back to the village much later, Carlo breathed deeply.

'No-one must ever know about this,' he said.

'It's OK,' said Stephany. 'No-one will. It's just one of those things that happened, isn't it? Only you and I know.'

Carlo felt terrible. He didn't want to hide anything from Ruth. But if he wanted to keep Ruth, he thought, he would have to hide it from her.

Chapter 10 *In love with two people*

The next morning Max got up before Stephany. She awoke to hear him moving across the room.

'I feel much better,' he said, looking at her. 'I've already been for a walk and bought us some things for breakfast. I'll make some more coffee.'

She lay and smelt the coffee and felt the warm sun on her face as it came through the window.

If yesterday hadn't happened, this could almost be the holiday she had wanted. But yesterday had happened. She didn't know what to think.

Carlo loved Ruth, he had told her that, and he would never leave her or the children. But he had always liked Stephany, too.

She looked up at Max as he gave her a cup of coffee. He looked extremely handsome this morning, and now he was better he seemed stronger. He was more like the Max she first knew and liked. Perhaps it was perfectly normal to be in love with two people at once?

'Here's a coffee for you,' he said, kissing her on the cheek. 'How was last night? Did you have a good time?'

'It was OK,' said Stephany. She had decided she would not tell Max that Ruth wasn't there, unless he asked. It was best to keep things simple.

'Did I miss anything?' Max asked.

'No,' said Stephany putting her arms around him. 'Nothing. But I missed you.'

Max smiled.

He really felt he was going to enjoy the rest of the holiday.

'How about taking the train to town? There's a market on today,' said Max, who had been talking to some tourists in the bar that morning. 'I could buy some fresh food and cook us a good meal this evening. There are also some interesting churches I'd like to look at.'

Stephany, who had been planning a day swimming and lying on the beach, did not want to go to town.

'Why don't you go alone?' she said. 'It'd be good for your Italian. I feel like lying in the sun with my book. Let's meet later on the beach.'

'Oh, OK,' said Max, 'I hope I'll be able to understand without you there to help me.'

'Of course you will,' said Stephany. 'Take the dictionary and use your hands a lot.'

So Stephany went to the beach and Max went to town on the train. He was pleased that he knew the Italian word for ticket – *biglietto*, but at the vegetable stall at the market he forgot the word for courgettes. He tried to find some courgettes to point to, but there weren't any. Then he tried to describe them but the man selling the vegetables couldn't understand him. Some people waiting became more and more angry.

'They are called *zucchini*,' said a voice behind him. Max turned round to find Ruth standing there. Thomas was holding her hand and the baby was in a pram.

'Oh, thank goodness you were there just then,' said Max. Then he told Ruth the vegetables he wanted and Ruth asked for them in perfect Italian.

'How was last night?' Max asked her as they left the vegetable stall.

'Last night?' Ruth didn't understand.

'The festival you and Carlo and Stephany went to while I was in bed.'

Ruth looked at Max. Didn't he know she hadn't gone? She thought quickly. If Stephany hadn't told Max, then she was trying to hide something. Ruth felt herself go red with anger. But she decided it was best not to tell Max now. She wanted to talk to Carlo first.

'It was fun,' said Ruth. 'Ask Stephany about it, I expect she would like to tell you.'

Max looked at Ruth, but she was now busy with Thomas. He decided Ruth didn't want to talk about last night. 'I'd like to buy some cheese. Would you help me?' he asked.

'Sure,' said Ruth, 'follow me. I know the best cheese stall here.' Max followed her to a stall with a lot of beautiful cheeses.

'We never get cheeses as big as this in England,' said Max. 'At the supermarkets everything is cut into tiny pieces and comes in plastic.'

'Oh yes,' said Ruth 'It's one of the things I love about Italy. Food is real food here.'

They bought some *Dolce Latte* and some *Pecorino*.

'And now for fruit,' said Max.

Ruth helped him choose some peaches and grapes, and then they walked around together for a while.

'Look at that church!' said Max. 'I must look inside. Would you like to?'

'Yes,' said Ruth. 'There are some pictures in there you might be interested in.' They went inside the church together, but it was a bit difficult to look at the pictures carefully with Thomas and the baby.

'It's nice to look at architecture and art with someone else,' said Max. 'Stephany isn't interested. We are very different. She likes sports while I like art. But I like the fact that we're different. How about you and Carlo?'

Ruth was quiet. She didn't want to talk about herself and Carlo right now. She was thinking about Stephany and didn't want to tell Max what she was thinking. She couldn't be sure that her thoughts about Stephany and Carlo were right. If she said anything to Max, he would think she was jealous of Stephany. After all, Stephany was far more attractive than she was.

'Would you like to go for a coffee?' asked Max, feeling sorry for Ruth again. She looked so tired.

'That'd be lovely,' she said, then turned to Thomas and said, 'Would you like an ice cream?'

'Sì, sì,' he shouted, running round them in circles. They found a cafe in the sun and sat outside. Max enjoyed playing with the little boy.

'He likes you,' laughed Ruth as Max made Thomas laugh. 'Have you and Stephany thought of having children yourselves?'

'We haven't been together very long,' he said. 'We haven't talked about it. But I don't think Stephany is very interested in having children yet. She enjoys her work, and she likes being free so much.'

'How about you?' Ruth asked.

'Well, I do like children. I've enjoyed playing with Thomas. But it's a big decision. I'm not sure I'm ready for it either.'

'I understand,' said Ruth. 'We've found it harder than we thought it would be. We don't get any time alone now.'

'How did you and Carlo meet? Were you already in Italy?' asked Max.

'Yes, I was working in a restaurant here. Carlo was one of my regular customers. He loves everything English, you know. He's an Anglophile! He was one of the few people I met who could speak English. Stephany taught him.'

'They never went out together?' Max asked.

'No,' said Ruth. She stopped for a moment.

'Stephany says they were just good friends,' said Max.

'They were,' said Ruth. 'When I met Carlo he told me all about how Stephany had taught him English and helped him in London. In return, he said she could use the flat whenever she wanted to. He's very kind.'

Max nodded. 'It's very kind of him. After all, he could make a lot of money from tourists out of it.'

'Carlo isn't like that,' said Ruth, smiling as she spoke of him. 'He doesn't do things to make money. He does things if they feel the right thing to do. That's what I love about him.'

Max looked at her as she smiled. She really loves Carlo, he thought. 'So Stephany and Carlo were never boyfriend and girlfriend?' Max asked again. He thought if anyone knew, Ruth would.

'No,' said Ruth. She kept her eyes down. She was speaking the truth, but she thought that perhaps it wasn't so simple. She couldn't tell Max that she didn't trust Stephany.

'Thanks for the coffee, Max. I must go now. I need to get home.'

Ruth called Thomas, moved the baby to her pram and took Thomas's hand. She turned and waved as she went to get her bus and Max noticed a sad look on her face.

'Poor woman,' he thought, 'she seems very tired all the time. She is not very happy living here. Even though it is so beautiful.'

Now he had heard from Ruth that Carlo and Stephany were just good friends and always had been, he felt much happier. He would really enjoy the rest of the holiday, and he would start right now. On the train back he thought of the nice meal he would cook tonight, with a bottle of good wine, and of being alone with his new woman at last.

Chapter 11 *The perfect holiday*

Max went back to the flat after his trip to town and prepared some food for the evening's meal. He wanted to make everything just right for Stephany now. He felt they had hardly seen each other alone since they left England and, after all, that was why they had come on holiday.

He put some wine in the fridge, got his swimming things, and went down through the quiet street. The smell of good food came from the houses on either side of the narrow street and Max smiled. This place was so wonderful. Every colour was brighter than in England, every sound clearer, every smell more delicious. He suddenly felt full of good feelings for everything and everyone.

Carlo and Ruth were so kind, he thought. They were good people and he was pleased to have two new friends. But right now he wanted to be alone with Stephany.

Max found Stephany asleep. She was lying on her front in a sunny corner of the beach. The clear water was only a few metres away. As it was early afternoon there was no-one else about. Most people had gone to cooler places or to restaurants to eat large lunches before sleeping all afternoon.

Seeing Stephany lying so sweetly in the sun, he thought how much he loved her. He had never felt like this before. He went quietly across the sand and sat down beside her.

She didn't move. He touched her back. Her skin felt hot and he thought she might be getting sunburn. Quietly he put a towel across her back and then lay down beside her. He put his arm across her shoulder and kissed her cheek. Her eyes opened. She looked at him for a few seconds, then smiled.

'Hello, darling,' she said.

'Hello, beautiful,' said Max.

She turned onto her side and put her head on his chest. This was a great holiday, he thought. A beautiful village, the sea, sun, a beautiful woman, and a good meal for them tonight.

Later in the afternoon they went swimming in the clear water. They swam out a little way and looked back at the pretty village from the sea.

'This is the perfect place for a holiday,' said Max. 'You were so clever to think of it.'

' I know,' said Stephany, and smiled.

Now she had had a good rest she felt better. She was beginning to forget about last night. No-one need ever know what had happened, and she wanted to enjoy being with Max.

'Let's come here for all our holidays,' said Max, as they swam back towards the beach. 'We'll get to know all the local people, and everyone will welcome us each year!'

Stephany laughed.

'You're too romantic,' she said.

'I know, but after all, Carlo has offered you the flat whenever you want it, so let's use it.'

'Mmmm,' said Stephany, and she suddenly went under the water and pulled Max's feet.

'You can't catch me!' she shouted when she came up, and then began swimming away from him. She was right. She was a much faster swimmer than Max was and she reached the beach first.

'Well, what do you think?' he asked when he finally reached the beach and sat down beside her, picking up her hand.

'About what?'

'About having more holidays together?'

'I think we should enjoy this one,' said Stephany. Max became worried that he was asking too much. Perhaps Stephany was not ready to get serious.

'By the way,' said Max. 'I met Ruth in town.'

Stephany looked up quickly. Had Ruth told him she hadn't gone to the festival?

But Max went on: 'Poor thing. She always looks so tired. Your late night last night at the festival didn't help.'

Stephany was pleased that Ruth hadn't told him that she wasn't there, but she also felt worried. What did Ruth know?

'Come on,' she said, wanting to talk about something else. 'Let's get dressed.'

The air was cooler by the time they got dressed and walked up to the hill path.

'Let's go for a drink in the bar,' said Max.

Stephany stopped for a moment. She didn't want to see Luigi in the bar. She was afraid of what he might say to her in front of Max.

'How about walking over to the next village, and finding a bar there?'

'Good idea,' said Max. 'There's a little church there I'd

like to have a look at. I heard about it from Ruth this morning.'

It was a beautiful walk with wonderful views of the blue sea below them and they could see tiny white sailing boats. They climbed up some steps to the next village and found themselves in a very pretty square.

On one side was a little church, which Max went to look at. Stephany found a table outside a bar and sat and watched the people come and go. She liked to look at the clothes the Italian women wore. They dressed very well. As she watched she thought about Luigi. He seemed to want to make trouble for her yesterday. And Stephany didn't want any more trouble this holiday. She was pleased they had come to a different bar.

Max soon came out of the church and sat down next to her. 'It's great,' he said. 'This tiny, unknown church is full of beautiful paintings. They would be in a museum in England, but here the paintings are allowed to stay where they were painted!'

Stephany reached over and took his hand. She thought he was very clever. They drank their drinks.

'What's the time?' Max asked. 'I need to start cooking or there won't be any dinner this evening!'

Stephany then realised her watch wasn't on her wrist.

'That's strange,' she said, 'I hope I didn't lose my watch when I was swimming this afternoon.'

'Oh, no,' said Max. 'We'd better look for it on the way home.'

They walked back looking out for Stephany's watch, but they couldn't find it.

'Never mind,' said Stephany. 'It might be in the flat. I don't remember putting it on today.'

Max put his arm round her.

'I'm making you a wonderful meal this evening,' he said. 'Then I think we should go to bed early. We'll worry about your watch tomorrow.'

'Mmmmmm,' said Stephany.

And that is exactly what they did.

Chapter 12 *A bad argument*

Life was not too easy for Ruth at the moment. She had to continue working at the restaurant to help pay some of the bills. She spent the day cooking food for the children, taking care of the baby, and reading Thomas stories. It was tiring and sometimes boring as well.

She wished she had more friends with children near by. She wished she got on better with Carlo's parents. She wished Carlo could get a job in England and she could go and live near her own family. But this was not possible at the moment.

At five o'clock that day she gave Thomas his tea and then gave him a bath. She was changing her clothes to go to work when Carlo came home. Ruth did not want an argument, but she wanted to ask about last night.

'Max didn't know that you and Stephany went to the festival alone,' she said. 'Why didn't she tell him?'

Carlo looked at her. 'I've no idea,' he said. 'How do you know she didn't tell him?'

'I met Max in town today, and he thought I was there last night,' she replied.

'Perhaps they hadn't had a chance to talk.'

Ruth looked hard at Carlo.

'Carlo. I want you to tell me the truth. Is Stephany trying to hide something?'

Ruth wanted to stay calm. She didn't want to get jealous

and angry. She wanted to believe Carlo. After all, he had told her Max was ill last night. If he had had something to hide, he wouldn't have told her. He had other women friends. She knew Carlo was not the kind of man to go with other women . . . unless he was pushed! And Stephany, Ruth couldn't help thinking, was the kind of woman who might push him.

'Let's not start all this again,' Carlo said.

He was afraid Ruth knew in her heart what had happened last night. He didn't want her to find out.

'But I don't understand!' Ruth went on. 'Why didn't Stephany tell Max she spent the evening with you at the festival?'

'How should I know?' asked Carlo, quite angry now. 'Ask Stephany if it's a problem for you!'

'Ask Stephany?' Ruth shouted. 'I don't want to ask Stephany! I hope I never have to speak to that woman again!'

'You are just jealous of her!' Carlo shouted, really angry now. 'You've always been jealous of her!'

'Yes, I have, because you were in love with her!' said Ruth.

Carlo's voice went quiet.

'I've got too many other problems at the moment to talk about this . . . I just hate it when you get jealous!'

Before she knew it, Ruth had picked up a cup and thrown it hard at Carlo. He moved his head and the cup flew past his ear.

'Watch out!' he shouted, as Ruth left the house angrily.

When she had gone, Carlo sat in his chair for a long time looking at the carpet.

He wished Stephany had never come back to Italy and

that he had not spent yesterday evening with her. Why had he done it? He was now really afraid Ruth would leave him.

It was much later when Ruth returned from her night's work at the restaurant.

'I'm sorry,' Ruth said. She'd had a chance to think, and she realised she was being stupid. Carlo and Stephany had always been good friends. She had to trust him. Carlo smiled, and put his arms round her.

'I'm sorry too,' he said. 'I just feel tired at the moment. But if it would help,' he said, 'I won't let Stephany use the flat again. It seems to make you so unhappy. And I want you to be happy.'

'It makes me sound so bad,' she said. 'But I just don't like Stephany, or believe her. I can't explain why.'

Carlo put his face in Ruth's hair. He felt he was going to cry. He wanted to tell her everything. But if he told her, she might leave him, and that was something he didn't want to think about.

Ruth felt good with Carlo's strong arms round her and she went to bed that night feeling better. But she would be happy only when Stephany had gone back to England. There was something about that woman that made Ruth very unhappy.

Chapter 13   *An unwanted invitation*

For Stephany and Max, the next two days were wonderful. They swam, ate good food and went for walks. Max visited more buildings and churches. Stephany was not interested in these so he often went on his own, while she sat at cafés with her book.

One day they went shopping in Genoa. Stephany bought some shoes and a new red dress. Max bought a new jacket.

'Italy is a wonderful country,' said Max. 'Good food, beautiful architecture, and great clothes as well.' He was enjoying this holiday more than he could have thought.

On their last afternoon Max said, 'This flat almost feels like home. I feel as though we've always lived here.' He didn't tell Stephany directly that he was enjoying living with her, but he had begun to think they should move in together when they went back to England. He was waiting for the right moment to talk about it.

Stephany had begun to think the same thing. The more she got to know Max, the more intelligent and more handsome she thought he was. He might not be the greatest swimmer and he had never been on water-skis, but he knew so much about architecture and art.

The days of their holiday passed quickly. They hadn't seen Carlo or Ruth again and Stephany began to relax; no-one would ever know about her evening with Carlo, she thought. In fact, she rather liked to remember the evening, and she thought of times in the future when she and Carlo would meet and make love. It was good to think she had a serious relationship with Max, a part-time lover in Carlo, and a beautiful flat to stay in, in Italy.

Max had never asked anything about the evening of the festival and Carlo had not phoned since then. She thought that Carlo understood it was best not to see each other at the moment.

On their last day in the village, Max decided he would take Stephany out that evening to an expensive restaurant he had seen near the beach. It would be the perfect place to ask her to move in with him when they got back to England.

Max felt sure that a beautiful sunset, a sea view and good food and wine would mean she couldn't say no.

But early that evening there was a knock on the flat door. It was Carlo's mother inviting them for a meal.

'I saw you earlier, eating in the bar, and I decided it was time you had a real Italian home-cooked meal,' she said.

Stephany thought for a moment. But she couldn't say no. The old woman would be hurt.

'Thank you,' said Stephany, 'that would be lovely.'

When the old woman had gone, Max looked at Stephany.

'What did she want?' he asked, although he thought he knew already.

'She's invited us for dinner this evening,' said Stephany, not looking at Max.

'And you accepted?'

'Well, I had to,' said Stephany. 'It wouldn't be nice to say no. She thinks we haven't been eating good food in the bars and restaurants.'

'How does she know?' asked Max, feeling angry.

'She's seen us,' said Stephany.

'But I wanted to take you for a meal at a really good restaurant,' said Max, feeling very angry.

'We can't say no,' said Stephany. 'She's Carlo's mother and we're staying in his flat. She'd be very hurt if we didn't want to go.'

Max knew Stephany was right. The trouble with being given something free, like a flat to stay in, was it meant you had to do things you didn't want to do sometimes.

You never really got anything free in this world, he knew that. There was always something to pay. And a meal with an old couple was a small price.

'Well, she's a very good cook,' said Stephany.

'Oh well,' said Max, 'we'll just have to try and enjoy it.'

They got ready for the evening. Stephany put on the red dress she had bought in town that week.

'You look beautiful,' said Max.

'You don't look too bad yourself,' said Stephany. Max was brown from the sun and it went well with his dark hair. He had put on his new jacket which made him look very handsome. Stephany felt very pleased.

To her surprise, when they went to the old couple's flat at seven o'clock, it was Carlo who opened the door.

'Oh,' said Stephany, her heart sounding so loud that she was afraid someone else might hear it. 'We didn't know you would be here.'

'It's my mother's house,' said Carlo. 'Naturally, she asked us to come too.'

'Hi!' Max said, happy that Ruth was there. He had thought everyone would be speaking in Italian all evening and he wouldn't understand a word of it.

'Come in,' said Carlo.

Ruth and the children were playing in the sitting room. Ruth was wearing jeans and a T-shirt. She looked very pretty tonight, Max thought.

Carlo stayed close to Ruth all evening. He put his arm round her and kissed her, and Ruth looked at him with her eyes full of love. It was as if Carlo was trying to show Stephany how well he and Ruth got on. He didn't talk much to Stephany.

Stephany tried not to think about it, but she couldn't help feeling bad – she knew she was looking attractive this evening and she wanted Carlo to say something. Max had said her dress made her look like a film star.

'Here, Thomas,' Carlo's mother was saying to the little boy. 'Have some chocolate!'

'But he hasn't had his dinner yet,' said Ruth. She had gone red with anger. Carlo's mother looked a little sad.

'OK,' Ruth said. 'Look, Thomas, *Nonna* wants to give you some chocolate.'

But Stephany could see Ruth didn't like Thomas having chocolate before dinner. 'How silly,' she thought. 'Just a little chocolate. Poor old woman! She just wants to be kind to her grandson!'

'What a lucky boy!' Stephany said, and Carlo's mother smiled at her. Ruth looked at Stephany angrily, but Stephany didn't notice.

'Let's eat!' said Carlo's mother, and they sat down at the table.

'You're a good swimmer,' Carlo's father said to Stephany as they sat round the table eating fresh pasta. Stephany looked at him, surprised. She didn't know he had seen her swimming.

'And you are very good at diving,' laughed Carlo's father. 'You're like one of the Italian boys!'

'Doesn't Max like diving?' asked Carlo's mother.

Goodness, thought Stephany, they have seen everything we have done since we arrived here. They know how we spend our days, and where we eat. What else do they know? she suddenly thought.

Chapter 14 *Back in the bar*

After the meal, Carlo asked if they wanted to go for a coffee at the bar. He wanted to get out of the flat. Ruth and his mother never got on, but it was worse with Stephany there, he thought. His mother seemed to like Stephany more and more, and that, he knew, was difficult for Ruth to watch.

'Thank you so much for a lovely meal,' Stephany said, kissing Carlo's mother on each cheek.

'It's nothing, my beautiful,' said the *Signora*. But Stephany noticed she didn't say goodbye to Ruth.

The two couples went down the narrow street to the bar, Thomas running ahead. Carlo carried the baby in his arms. Carlo and Ruth looked like the perfect couple tonight.

Seeing Carlo for the first time since their evening together, Stephany found she still wanted him. But he was not looking at her at all. They sat round a table in the bar and Luigi took their orders. Luigi was a different character tonight. He was friendly and funny with Carlo, he liked Ruth, and he played with Thomas.

Finally Carlo said, 'Well, we must be going.' He had his arm round Ruth. 'We probably won't see you two again,' he said. 'You're leaving tomorrow, aren't you? So it's goodbye.'

'That's strange,' thought Stephany. 'It sounds as if he's

saying goodbye for the last time. What does he mean by "we won't see you again?"'

Carlo held out his hand and shook Max's hand.

'It's been good meeting you,' he said.

'And you,' said Max. 'And I can't thank you enough for the flat. Of course, I should thank Stephany too, for being your friend in the first place.' Stephany looked away. 'I hope we'll meet again one day,' said Max. 'Perhaps you could all come and stay with us in England.'

There was a difficult silence.

'One day, maybe,' said Carlo.

Then they all kissed each other goodbye, and Ruth and Carlo disappeared up the street.

'Let's have one more drink,' Max said to Stephany. 'I feel like staying out late tonight. We've hardly had any time alone together this holiday.'

'OK,' said Stephany. She was no longer worried about Luigi. After all, he had been so friendly this evening.

Stephany ordered a hot chocolate and Max ordered a glass of brandy. They sat at one of the tables outside. A light wind blew things about the street, and once it blew over the empty bottles on their table.

'The weather's changing,' said Max. A lot of people had gone inside the bar, away from the light rain which had begun to fall. They could hear waves crashing onto the rocks below.

'I was thinking,' Max said, looking at Stephany across the table and taking her hand. 'It's been such a lovely week here, we've got on so well. Better in some ways than in London. How would you feel about moving in together when we get back?'

Stephany looked at Max. She was still thinking about Carlo's final words. So suddenly she felt happy she had Max. After all, he was far more handsome than Carlo.

'Oh, Max,' she said, kissing him. 'I 've been thinking the same thing.'

Just then, Luigi came over to take their empty glasses. He stopped, his hands full, then spoke in English. 'I expected to see you at the festival the other night. Where were you?'

Max laughed. 'I was ill in bed,' he said, 'but Stephany was there, with Carlo and Ruth.'

'No,' said Luigi, looking at Stephany now. 'They were not there. I looked out all evening for Carlo and he wasn't there. And when I asked Ruth, she said she stayed at home with Thomas.'

Max looked at Stephany. 'Where were you?' he asked. 'I never asked what you did that evening.'

'Oh,' said Stephany, 'Carlo and I decided not to go to the festival. We decided it wouldn't be fun without you and Ruth.'

'By the way,' Luigi said, 'I found this on Bianca Beach.' And he gave something to Stephany. It was her watch.

'I found it on Wednesday morning,' said Luigi. 'Well, goodbye.' And he went off looking very pleased with himself.

'Bianca Beach?' Max asked, suddenly feeling rather uncomfortable. 'Have we been to Bianca Beach?' He knew they hadn't, and wasn't sure why he was asking.

'I don't like that waiter,' Stephany said angrily. 'He's got a bad look about him. Come on, I've finished my drink. Let's go.'

'Wait,' said Max. 'If you and Carlo weren't at the festival, and Ruth wasn't with you, then you must have been at Bianca Beach. Why didn't you tell me?'

Stephany began to feel a little frightened. She looked up at Max, trying to think of something to say.

'I hope it's not what I'm thinking,' said Max, suddenly feeling very jealous. 'You didn't . . . you and Carlo . . . I don't believe this!'

'Hey Max,' said Stephany. She was frightened now. Max was not going to forget this if he found out the whole truth.

'Don't start getting jealous!'

But this time, Max knew he wasn't being jealous for nothing.

'How could you?' shouted Max. 'Carlo's got a wife and children!'

'Why don't you say "How could *he*?"' said Stephany back to him, suddenly very angry. 'It takes two, you know!'

'Because I don't care what he does. I care what you do!' Max shouted.

'Shhh!' said Stephany. 'Everyone's looking at us. Let's go. We can talk somewhere else.'

As they got up to leave Stephany realised for the first time why Ruth hated living in a small village. It was as if everyone knew everything about her, and were never going to let her forget it.

They walked towards the beach without talking. The waves were really big now and they could hear thunder in the distance. Then Stephany said, 'Max, you must understand, it means nothing to me now.'

'We're talking about two days ago,' said Max. 'How can

you do something one day, and then say it means nothing two days later?'

Stephany couldn't answer.

'Were you always lovers?' asked Max, remembering now his thought that it would be difficult for any man to be 'just good friends' with Stephany.

'Only once,' said Stephany. 'I was telling you the truth when I said we were just friends when he offered me his flat the first time.'

'So when were you lovers before?' asked Max.

'Two years ago, the first time I met Ruth, there was an evening . . .'

'You mean you waited until Carlo was married to Ruth before deciding to sleep with him?' Max was beginning to understand and he didn't like what he was learning about Stephany.

'I was afraid I was going to lose him,' said Stephany.

'But . . . but, you had already lost him!' said Max. 'He was married to Ruth.'

'Oh! You are so stupid,' shouted Stephany. 'The trouble with men,' she said, 'is there is always one rule for them, and a different one for women. These things happen, you know!' Then she turned and ran off into the night.

Chapter 15   *Lovers or friends?*

It was Saturday evening, but Stephany had nowhere to go. She sat on the sofa, looking at the telephone. Max had not spoken to her on the flight home, and at Stansted Airport he had kissed her goodbye and gone to get a train. A week had passed, and he had not telephoned her. How could a holiday end so badly? she wondered. It had all been going so well with Max before the holiday.

She thought about their last evening in Italy. It seemed a million years ago now. Max had asked her to live with him! And now he wasn't speaking to her. She wanted to cry. She had had a bad week. She couldn't help thinking about Carlo. If she had never kissed him that evening, they would still be friends.

Now she felt she had no-one, no friend, and no lover. She picked up the phone and, although she thought Max was probably not at home, she called his number. She waited. Finally he answered.

'Max?' she said, before he could speak. 'I love you, please believe me!'

Max didn't say anything for a few seconds, then said, 'I can't.'

'Well, at least, Max, can we still be friends?'

'Just friends?' asked Max.

'Yes,' said Stephany. 'Just good friends.'

To her surprise, Max started to laugh. 'Do you know what a good friend is?' he asked.

'Of course I do, I've got lots of good friends,' said Stephany.

'Including Carlo?' Max said.

'Carlo was a good friend. But . . . we destroyed it. I understand that now. I feel so lonely. Last week you were both my friends. Now I've got neither of you!' There was a silence. Was Max feeling sorry for what had happened?

'Stephany,' he said. 'I'll tell you what a good friend is. A good friend is someone who is honest with you.'

'OK, Max,' said Stephany. 'Maybe I'm not good at being "good friends", but you know we were good lovers. Didn't you enjoy being with me?'

'Yes, I did,' said Max, sadly, 'but it's over, Stephany. I can't have a relationship with a woman I can't trust.'

'You can trust me,' said Stephany. 'I promise I shall never let it happen again.'

'It's too late,' said Max. 'I'm sorry . . .'

Stephany put the phone down. She wanted to cry. Then suddenly she felt angry. If it wasn't for her, Max wouldn't have had a holiday at all. It wasn't fair that she should be left with nothing. She went and looked in the mirror.

'Well, perhaps not nothing,' she thought, looking at herself in the mirror. 'I still look pretty, and I've still got other friends.' She picked up the phone again. She called a friend, a woman this time, and asked her if she wanted to meet her in a club later that night. She then put on her red dress, made up her face, and went out of her flat.

She didn't need Carlo and Max, she thought. Tonight was Saturday night. She wasn't going to sit at home all evening feeling sorry for herself. She was going out to have a good time.